# THE
# SELF REPAIR
# TOOLKIT

## Empowering the Self

## DEBORAH SMALL

British Columbia, Canada

DEBORAH SMALL

DEDICATION

This manual is dedicated to all the teachers who inspired me towards the path of Love and Self Realization.

DEBORAH SMALL

# ACKNOWLEDGEMENTS

There are so many people who have made this manual a possibility.

Firstly, to my parents Martin and Mona Cay without whom I would not be here.

My husband Ian, without whom this manual would not exist as he was the one who pushed me to create it.

My children Lyndall, Morgan and Victoria for choosing me, I am forever grateful for the experience and honour of being a mother, without which I could not be who I am today.

My teacher Bikram Choudhry who created the best therapeutic healing yoga sequence in the world, guiding me towards a healthy body, mind, and spirit, without which this manual would not be possible.

My teacher Sri Sri Ravi Shankar, for teaching me that I am responsible for everything that happens in my life. "With total responsibility comes total freedom". Without this knowledge I could not produce this manual, as it was born from my own experience.

To my fellow yoga teachers and IRT facilitators, too many to mention. Without your love and encouragement this manual would not come into being. "Never give up".

Lastly, to everyone who has ever trusted me to be their teacher/facilitator without your faith in me this manual would not be possible. I am honoured that I could play a small part on your journey towards freedom.

DEBORAH SMALL

RED APPLE
PUBLISHING

# The Self Repair Toolkit

## INDEX

# FOREWORD

*Welcome to the* **Self Repair Toolkit***. Thank you for taking the profound step in deciding to go through this very personal journey using the powerful, yet simple and effective tools provided here.*

*My name is* **Deborah Small***. I am a qualified and experienced Integrative Reprogramming Technique [IRT] Practitioner. IRT is a science-based self-treatment methodology that comprises very simple, yet powerful tools to create permanent change within you. The* **Self Repair Toolkit** *was designed and compiled for people just like me and you.*

*Clients from across the world had asked me many times if there was some material available that they could access or have to help them in their understanding and for their life journey. This* **Self Repair Toolkit** *was born of that need.*

*The approach that is used here is an adapted IRT derivative process that is individual-focused. That means, it lends itself to working on one person at a time. It is a very personal journey to go through. It is entirely about "You", working with, "You". In the physical absence of a skilled IRT Facilitator, the* **Self Repair Toolkit** *provides you with the simple tools needed to successfully progress through the entire process.*

*At your own speed, pacing yourself; take the full amount of time necessary to properly apply each tool. Some tools may prove quick to execute and deal with for you; some may prove to be long and drawn out. I strongly advise that you stay the course and see the process through to completion; it's truly worth understanding yourself better. The benefits of this process are manifold; creating & enhancing personal congruency both internally and externally.*

# ADVANCE PRAISE

*"Working with Deb helped me heal a lot of fear that I didn't know how to deal with. I felt lighter and better every time we met. Deb knows how to read people and to help them with whatever it is they are dealing with. Highly recommend!"*
— *Julie*

*"When I met Deb I was very chaotic, worried, and unbalanced. I was not handling or accepting the circumstances in my life very well at all. Deb had a way of calming me energetically and assisting me to change my beliefs on so many levels. Much of what I learned from Deb, I still use today. Deb's sessions are deep and impactful. One of the most valuable experiences of my life".*
— *Geoff*

*"Deborah is highly skilled in assisting you to get at the root of what is and is not working across all areas of your life and health. Her approach and toolkit empowers you in a straightforward, no fluff manner to take responsibility in creating your best life. The techniques Deb employs to facilitate and support healing are profoundly effective. Be prepared for transformation!"*
— *Janice*

*"I call Deb Small my 'life changer'. Over time, Deb has introduced me to tools that have helped me develop a new dimension of consciousness. It has not been easy to look at my own personal patterns, convoluted preferences, and unrealistic expectations, but I have done so, with Deb's help. After much effortless effort, soul searching and tears, (and some laughter too), I am starting to take responsibility for my life. With total responsibility, comes total freedom. The journey to self-love and acceptance brings inner peace and happiness, and Deb is a living example of this".*
— *Jessie*

*"When I went to see Deb I was unhappy with the relationships I had with individuals in my life. I had suffered with depression in the past, and always seemed to have stress and anxiety about finances or just life. During Deb's sessions she helped teach me how to change my thinking, let go of guilt, live in the present, and find my own happiness. I have learned to let go of the past, not worry about the future, and to experience all kinds of emotions by allowing them to pass through me without getting stuck. Thank you, thank you, thank you, Deb. Now I am happy and have found a balanced path through life. I would, and have, highly recommended Deb as an alternative to traditional counselling".*
— *Tracey*

# INTRODUCTION

Hello and thank you for deciding to be here. You've made a conscious choice. It's THE choice. You have chosen to address those things within your life, within you, that don't fit with your picture of reality; that don't conform with your ideal state of self; that make you uncomfortable, unhappy or sad much of the time. Now here you are, ready to do something about that.  So, what next?

Well, let me deal with the impact question right up front. The one that cuts to the chase:

## "Does this really work?"

## Yes!     Absolutely!

All it takes is…     **You!**

For the **Self Repair Toolkit** to be effective, it only needs one missing ingredient to be added. That's a willing you. And here you are.

The **Self Repair Toolkit** is a series of tools designed by world-renowned Integrated Reprogramming Technique & Yoga Practitioner, Deborah Small, with the purpose of providing everyone with a straight-forward set of simple, easy-to-use tools to deal with key parts of life's challenges & problems. It addresses the perceived complexities and issues surrounding the 'Self'.

The **Self Repair Toolkit** takes key elements of the Integrated Reprogramming Techniques [IRT] and combines these with knowledge gathered from nearly three decades of research & practice into a simplified, easy-to-use and to easy-to-apply process. You follow the process using each tool in sequence; it delivers the result. It is proven to work with committed users.

**"Does this work for everybody?"** The **Self Repair Toolkit** addresses your personal barriers and deals directly with each individual's own issues within its uniquely robust framework. Anyone can use the **Self Repair Toolkit**. It works if you follow the steps.

The Toolkit comprises an overall process, including analysis exercises, the application of specific tools to each component of the process, and an evaluation of the results. It's a remarkably easy process to follow. The tools are readily understandable and make total sense. The key ingredient to the process is your complete honesty with yourself.

This process works right down to a molecular and sub-atomic level. Your honesty removes the cellular 'muscle-memory' reactiveness imbedded in each of us that holds you back through involuntary repeated pattern behaviours, which can keep you trapped in your problems and misery.

**Process:** The process encompasses a series of tools in the form of exercises that require you to affirm to yourself that you will depart from your past thinking patterns and behaviours. You undertake a journey to establishing a new set of thinking patterns and behaviours that best fits you now, divesting of redundant elements in your life that no longer serve you.

## Twelve Tools

TOOL ONE — **WHY AM I HERE/DOING THIS?**

TOOL TWO — **LIFE STORY**

TOOL THREE — **TWENTY DISLIKES**

TOOL FOUR — **TEN LIKES**

TOOL FIVE — **TRIGGERS IDENTIFICATION**

TOOL SIX — **TRIGGERS EVALUATION**

TOOL SEVEN — **TRIGGERS RELEASE**

TOOL EIGHT — **BARRIERS RECOGNITION**

TOOL NINE — **BELIEF SYSTEMS**

TOOL TEN — **WHO AM I?**

TOOL ELEVEN — **PERMISSIONS**

TOOL TWELVE — **VISIONING**

Each tool in the process involves a commitment from you to tackle each task and question fully and openly from the heart.

These process-driven tools, in essence, form the Self Repair Toolkit. It is this 'Journey to the Self', starting at a departure point that requires totally honest self-acknowledgement and progressing to an arrival point where you uncover your true 'Self' in each moment.

The **Self Repair Toolkit** process takes you through a sequential flow of twelve applied thinking tools.

# SELF REPAIR TOOLKIT
# PROCESS TOOLS SUMMARY

**TOOL ONE - WHY AM I HERE/DOING THIS:** It commences with your very own Affirmation Statement. This requires you to state to yourself that you truly believe that you need to go through this exercise. "Why am I here? Why am I doing this?"

**TOOL TWO - MY LIFE STORY:** The toolkit then requires you to lay out a synopsis of your own life story, from start to present.

**TOOLS THREE & FOUR - DISLIKES & LIKES:** The toolkit then asks you to engage with two framing tools; it asks you to candidly lay out what you perceive are the disliked and liked traits about yourself. All recognized and recorded in the moment of each exercise.

**TOOLS FIVE, SIX & SEVEN - TRIGGERS:** This brings you around to identifying and confronting the Triggers in your life. Triggers are those elements and aspects which come at you from third parties that your own paradigms instantly react to, in a deeply embedded pre-determined manner. Through these process tools you learn to evaluate each Trigger and to ultimately release yourself from its invisible grip.

**TOOL EIGHT - BARRIERS:** You transition to recognizing the barriers in your life that prevent you from moving forward or dealing with those aspects that create the chaos and concern you experience on a daily basis.

**TOOL NINE - BELIEF SYSTEMS:** Having wrestled with and dealt with the Triggers inherent in your daily life, you are ready to move on to dealing with your deep-seated Belief Systems. This comprises the manifold ideas, value sets, cultural frameworks and activity-linked behaviours that you have embedded within yourself over the years, from childhood through to the present.

These Belief Systems govern how you deal with life and essentially control how you navigate through life's experiences. They are a set of pre-programmed behaviours mapped to most circumstances you will encounter in your world. Sadly, not all of these work to the benefit or to the good of the carrier. This is why we deal with them in this journey-to-Self, as a separate tool in the Self Repair Toolkit process.

**TOOL TEN - WHO AM I?:** From the picture you portray from Likes/Dislikes, you ask the fundamental question of yourself; 'is this me?' This forms part of the 'Who am I?' process tool and is a pivotal element of the journey-to-Self. Facing this fundamental question honestly and with personal congruency empowers you like never before. It will also provide you with tremendous impetus in moving forward through the remaining process tools.

**TOOL ELEVEN - PERMISSIONS:** The penultimate process tool involves addressing the condition of 'Permissions'. This explores the nature of Permissions and how they affect you in your daily life. When you learn how to deal with these, you no longer unconsciously abrogate or give up power over yourself to any others.

**TOOL TWELVE - VISIONING:** The final process tool is one which involves visioning for the future. It is optional. Not everyone is ready to delve into looking ahead so soon after arriving at their own true Self. Others cannot wait to explore the future and its possibilities right away. It'll be your choice.

# TOOL # 1

## WHY AM I HERE/DOING THIS?

This is about establishing your purpose. Asking this question is a very good way of anchoring the whole process of Self repair.

More than just asking "why am I here?" it is asking you to come to grips with "what is my true purpose?" Search your inner Self and take at least twenty minutes to address this fundamental question.

Many people arrive at this point in their lives. It's at that point when you question why things in your life are the way they are and why you're feeling the way you feel. Often they experience it multiple times.

Some feel tired of life; some are at a low point, lacking energy and/or creativity. Some people come to a realization that their path through life keeps leading them along the same old road, resulting in them falling down the same "rabbit-hole", over and over, without deviation.

Many come to this juncture in their lives through relationships that prove unfulfilling or even toxic, or are failing without discernible reasons. Others actively seek this departure point through driving forces such as fear and anxiety in their life.

It really doesn't matter what actually brought you to this point. Whether it's regret, rejection, anger, addiction, confusion, depression, grief; all of these are symptoms of why people arrive here. They are just that; symptoms. Symptoms of why people want to change their life. All of the people that arrive in this same spot that you find yourself ask the exact same questions of themselves; "How can I change this? What must I do to get things to change?" However, we must realize that these symptoms are also gifts. For without these circumstances we would never be challenged to look for something different or something better within ourselves. They allow us to explore aspects within ourselves that were previously hidden within us. After all, isn't that our purpose; to explore our gifts? What we have to offer to the world, to ourselves.

**AFFIRMATION STATEMENT**

**EXERCISE:**

**Take the next twenty minutes to write down "WHY AM I HERE/DOING THIS?"**

**I am here because…**

Now that you have established why you are here, you can proceed to Tool Two, 'My Life Story'.

# TOOL # 2

## MY LIFE STORY.

This is a chapter-by-chapter story about your life so far.

Starting as far back as you can go, within twenty minutes [not more], give a summary of your life to date: Starting with your birth, including parents and siblings and moving on from there.

**WHAT TO DO: This tool is about you taking a snapshot retrospective look at yourself:** Write down what you believe your life story to be; in your own words. Compose it as if you were to tell it to a complete stranger. Be honest and forthright. Again, take no more than twenty minutes to do it, but be sure to complete it. This timing is important. It requires you to focus on the predominant aspects of your life story.

**WHY DO IT: It allows you to distance yourself from the perceived 'You' that you hold in your mind. It gets you to re-evaluate the picture of who you believe yourself to be.**

'My Life Story' is an exercise that facilitates your eventual disengagement from your past profile traits. The telling of 'My life Story' frees you to give voice to your journey to the now and to being the person you believe yourself to be; all as a direct result of taking that journey.

By doing this, then repeating the result of your Life Story to yourself over and over, it can begin to have you identify less and less with that story.

'So why would I want to identify less with my own personal journey; my life's story?" you probably are wondering.

Well, that's a great question. It speaks to the necessity of trying actively and consciously to disconnect yourself in the now, from those elements of your past that you have dragged along with you in your life's journey. Many of them are no longer relevant to your current living or life's purpose.

That is to say, your Life Story is <u>too</u> caught up in the past, because over time you have assimilated all those acquired characteristics and have embedded those behaviours deep within you and you continue to live your life through using them. Many of those acquired Life Story behaviours probably served you well in years gone by, but are in need of being released by you. By releasing them, you will allow newer, more relevant ones to take their place. It becomes a process of reconnecting yourself to the present.

You know, you can put so much ownership into your Life Story that you are almost compelled to relive it and reinforce it over and over. Much of your past experiences no longer add to you in the present, in your current circumstances. Let go.


**EXERCISE:**

**My given name is… I was born on/at…**

# TOOL # 3

## TWENTY TRAITS I DISLIKE ABOUT MYSELF

This exercise will help you to identify many hidden traits about yourself.

You have 'permission' to boldly write down twenty traits about yourself that you don't like. These encompass traits that are physical, behavioral, emotional, etc.

Don't overthink it. Just list the first twenty that pop into your head.

The reason we put this in as a tool, is because many of us never get 'permission' to admit that we have traits that we don't like; that we perhaps wish we could change or eradicate.

You have permission to have qualities which are not-so-admirable; there are a few reasons for this. When you openly show that negative traits do exist in you, you can also give them permission to be released from you.

Negative traits in our society are often frowned upon; they are not readily accepted by others. However, this doesn't mean that they don't exist within us. So, what we tend to do is hide them, or repress them, and unfortunately, because of this, they fester. Sometimes they fester so much we blow up and we do unwanted or bad things.

Giving yourself permission to be okay with your 'bad' traits and bringing them to the forefront is what will help you to transform them. Denying that you have negative traits keeps them trapped within you. Acknowledging and accepting your negative traits is the best thing you can do for yourself. So go ahead, you have permission.

**EXERCISE:** Without overthinking it, right now in this moment, write down twenty traits about yourself that you do not like:

1...................................................................................................................

2...................................................................................................................

3...................................................................................................................

4...................................................................................................................

5...................................................................................................................

6...................................................................................................................

7...................................................................................................................

8...................................................................................................................

9...................................................................................................................

10.................................................................................................................

11.................................................................................................................

12.................................................................................................................

13.................................................................................................................

14.................................................................................................................

15.................................................................................................................

16.................................................................................................................

17.................................................................................................................

18.................................................................................................................

19.................................................................................................................

20.................................................................................................................

## WHAT TO DO WITH THEM:

Once you have completed these, it is quite possible that you may experience a contraction of your spirit within yourself. For many of us, looking at our negative qualities/darker images proves to be uncomfortable. However, it is imperative that you are accepting of these qualities in order to transcend them.

Take a few moments to be with each of these qualities, to openly accept them and to show compassion for yourself. These qualities can teach us valuable lessons about who we are. Therefore, in order to become whole, or to feel whole, it's in our best interest to make peace with these.

This process, remember, might take a long time. The idea behind it is that when one becomes aware, change can happen. So do not be worried if you cannot resolve or face all the negative qualities in one go; this is your own process. It will take as long as it needs to go through it. A minute, an hour, a day, a week, a month, or more; the timing is unique to you. Take as long as it requires.

Also, remember that the negatives can change from day to day. Some replace others, some fall away, others are added. It's fluid. Life happens.

The main thing to consider is to face them with compassion, acceptance and even thankfulness for the learning to be had from them.

Try this exercise after completing this list: select the three traits that you dislike the most about yourself and examine them. Whatever discomfort arises, allow yourself to feel that. If necessary or needs be, forgive yourself for when you were hurt or hurt someone else through the manifestation of those traits.

Keeping your eyes closed, sit for a moment, and say out loud; "**I forgive myself**." Breathe, then wait a moment, giving every cell in your body time to respond to your statement and release any negative blocked energy stored in your cells. Use the exhalation of your breath as a release valve until the intensity of the feeling(s) caused by the negative traits dissipates. You can use this releasing technique with all negative traits over time.

Now you are ready for Tool #4.

# TOOL # 4

## TEN TRAITS I LIKE ABOUT MYSELF

Writing down ten good traits about yourself allows you to feel expanded through joy felt from within. This exercise is a 'feel-good' after the heavy exercise of twenty dislikes, which creates contraction within a person.

It has proved itself to be an invaluable tool in setting and creating a positive framework view of the Self.

The Ten Likes paint a unique positive picture of you that you immediately connect to. This recording and portrayal of your likes heightens your awareness of and, directly connects you to your 'upside'.

It gets you associating with your identifiable positive and likeable qualities. It gets you looking at the "glass half-full".

By doing this, it frees you to apply the same thought to others; it has you actively looking for the 'Likes' in other people. Allowing such a very positive outlook and approach seep into your life view often creates a very positive and uplifting ripple effect in both you and those around you.


**EXERCISE:**

Right now, in this moment, without over-thinking; write down ten traits you like about yourself – no more, no less:

1..........................................................................................................

2..........................................................................................................

3..........................................................................................................

4..........................................................................................................

5..........................................................................................................

6..........................................................................................................

7..........................................................................................................

8..........................................................................................................

9..........................................................................................................

10........................................................................................................

## WHAT TO DO WITH THEM:

Now that you have completed the exercise, it is important to identify with each one. That means you should start to fully embrace these qualities.

Take a few moments, with eyes closed, to focus on each point individually and explore the experience of how the positive quality makes you feel.

In that process, try to become aware of each and every cell in your body, with gratitude to yourself. It's very much a feel-good experience.

Get in touch.

Connect to the **expansion** of your Self.

When you focus on your perceived positive qualities, it has a tendency to create yet more positive qualities. They unfold before you, as you accept each one after the other.

# TOOL # 5

## TRIGGERS IDENTIFICATIONS

Tool Five in the Self Repair Toolkit brings you to a very important part of the Self repair process. Each SRT Tool is a key component, but this one is crucial to your successful progress.

In Tool #5 we begin to look at Triggers. It's very important to identify what Triggers are and why they affect our daily lives. Many of us completely miss this aspect of Triggers.

### 1.  What are Triggers?

At times, we'll meet people who have the ability to trigger mainly negative emotions within us. For example, harsh words from someone who is disrespecting you, with the result that you experience feelings of hurt, which brings forth a negative emotion within you.

The key to understanding Triggers is to know that these kinds of emotion are ever-present within each and every one of us and therefore, are our responsibility. We own them. Whenever we take full responsibility over such emotions, we can start to change them within a positive framework. However, failure to take responsibility over these emotions transfers power over them from the Self, to the people capable of triggering these same emotions – and none of us has any real power to compel anyone else to change. So these emotions prevail.

## 2. How to identify Triggers

Recall events in your life where/when you have experienced these triggers. Write them down. Make a list. Identify them. Now, own them. Take full responsibility for them. They only affect you if you give up or abrogate permission and power over them. That's the responsibility aspect. When you acknowledge that you alone have created and empowered these triggers, taking full responsibility over them gives you more freedom in your life.

This exercise helps you to take responsibility over your triggered emotions and allows you to transform them.

All of us contain set responses to specific events, happenings, circumstances. These responses help us navigate through life and manoeuver over the unexpected bumps and pitfalls in our life journey.

There are, however, those specific things, or behaviours of others, that can automatically elicit a negative response from you or within you. They can bring out unwanted and disliked behaviours and feelings, leaving you down or despairing inside.

Please take ten minutes now to go through your mind's memories and try to recall some of these types of scenarios that have happened in your life. Write down the two most disliked or disturbing ones.

When you have them in front of you, examine them as if you are another person viewing them from a neutral standpoint. Try to identify what a more measured or appropriate and reasonable response could be or have been for each.

Now look at them in terms of why you respond the way you do, or did. What specifically prompts you to act in that manner? Do you believe it to be another person or thing causing you to behave in that way?

If you answered 'yes' to this last question, then you need to understand that your own true Self is being negated.

Any Trigger is, and can only ever be, a manifestation of you.

Only you can bestow power to an action of another or a thing that can hurt or harm you. Engaging in accusatory behaviours or assigning blame to others for those particular circumstances is to miss the reality of what is actually taking place.

When you can take responsibility for the moment, only then can you begin to understand that the negativity you have associated with the Trigger and the unwanted or disliked responses from yourself are all caused by you, not by anyone else or anything else.

By embedding a dislike or anathema to a specific activity, thing or behaviour within you and linking it to an offensive or defensive behaviour by yourself, you have effectively created your own problem

Recognizing that you are the true architect of these Triggers, that you have created and authored them wholly and solely for a purpose of making yourself a victim, is a step towards releasing your Self from all these Triggers-related behaviours.

You dislike them. They make you feel uncomfortable, yet you engage in them repeatedly. You need to make a conscious effort to take back power over your Self.

That means you cease to allow set responses to 'Trigger' events to prevail over, or dominate your behaviour.

De-victimize your Self. It's a big healing step, but you can do it. When you can say to your Self in complete honesty, "I'm responsible for all of it" and mean it, that's when you have taken back power over your own true Self.

We need to be able to identify what constitutes a problem before we can address it and affect change. Problem identification and recognition assists us in accepting responsibility for these essentially 'Trigger' moments and situations.

We know that many Triggers are vested in learned behaviours. They are often the types of action-response that were dealt with perhaps years before in a certain manner that proved appropriate to circumstances back then. However, as each of us progresses through life and becomes more than we were previously, it is often appropriate to let go of old behaviours in favour of newer, more comfortable ones.

Recognizing these behaviours related to Triggers and consciously determining to change or discard them is a huge step towards healing and revitalization of the Self.

**EXAMPLE:**

> Sally & Jack have been going steady for two years. They are very much in love and looking forward to spending the rest of their lives together. Everything is going well. However, Sally likes to shop and buy things that she really doesn't need, nor can afford.
>
> Jack has noticed this over the months and is uncomfortable with it, but doesn't want to say anything because he doesn't want to rock the boat of their relationship. After all, she is the girl of his dreams. Now, if she could only stop spending. But, the spending continues and Jack becomes more and more distressed by it. A significant fear is consequently triggered in Jack, as he doesn't feel he can commit to the rest of his life with a person who cannot control her spending habits. Jack is now conflicted.
>
> **Jack breaks up with Sally.**
> Now, this might have been a good reason to break up with Sally, but if Jack had only talked to Sally about his triggered fear, instead of pretending everything was okay, then perhaps they could have worked through that. However, as he saw her behaviour as the problem and not his triggered fear as being the problem, he was unable to reach any resolution of the issue.
>
> One day, out of the blue [for Sally], Jack says he is leaving and he doesn't want to be with her any more. He moves on with his life and begins dating someone else. Obviously, there are many things that can be said about this scenario, but we are focusing on the Triggers.
>
> This fear about money, or debt was very deeply hidden within Jack. When Sally was just being herself, she triggered this within

Jack, without knowing she had done so. Instead of Jack acknowledging the situation and taking responsibility for his fears, he decides to rather 'get out', which was a 'safer' course of action for him than facing his fear.

So, going forward, Jack carries with him the same unresolved fear that will no doubt encounter another similar trigger. He is fated to repeat the behaviour in similar circumstances. He has opted for temporary relief as opposed to dealing with the root cause of his fear, as he was unaware of why he acted the way he did in response to Sally's behaviours. Being aware of Triggers and what they are can help us all to deal with our fears and challenges and can make us aware that they are our own responsibility. Through this approach of openly recognizing one's Triggers and taking ownership of them, we become free of their effect on us. Taking total responsibility creates total freedom in one's life. It's not always the easy way, but it's a proven way that works, leading to long-term benefits.

**EXERCISE:**

Take twenty minutes to identify your triggers.

**My Triggers are...**

# TOOL # 6

## TRIGGERS EVALUATION

Take time now to look at the Triggers you have listed. Examine them in depth. Ask yourself, why do these particular things trigger you?

As you look closer into them, you will begin to recognize that some will have come from your early life, some from your environment/society.

Ask Yourself:
- Does holding on to these triggers help me in any way to move forward in my life?
- Are these triggers affecting my health [mental/spiritual/physical/emotional]?
- Am I willing to change my mind?
- Am I willing to let go of the past?
- Am I willing to show up now, in my life?

By going through this exercise you are able to evaluate your own responsibility to yourself, with regards to what triggers you. It will empower you to recognize these as they arise and transform them into non-impactful statements.

You now have an understanding of what constitutes Triggers, and have specifically identified some of the Triggers that affect you directly.

The Self Repair Toolkit Tool asks you to take the Triggers that you know impact you and to evaluate each of them. The individual evaluation of each is in terms of the effect of their impacts.

Are they all negative, or are there some positive impact Triggers. Do they make you feel good or bad, or perhaps both?

Once you have written down how each Trigger impacts you, it is time to step back and evaluate each of them. This is done in terms of what you would consider as possible alternatives to the Triggers-related behaviours that you have instinctively displayed to date. Think of how each Trigger situation could be handled or responded to differently. Differently, in a way that leaves you in a neutral or positive mind-set and spirit.

Now, write down possible alternatives next to your usual responses. Ask your Self, "How can I replace the Old with the New?"

This needs to be an honest assessment of what you know deep down inside you is really possible to replace the embedded behaviours.

You may be concerned that you may not have it within you to source alternate responses. Give it enough time for you to come up with specific replacement behaviour for each of them. Be sure in your heart that these proposed new behaviours represent the authentic "You" and know that they will leave you in a better condition than what they are replacing.

# TOOL # 7

## TRIGGERS RELEASE

Triggers are based upon old habits, behavioural patterns and deep-seated belief systems [paradigms]. What is required for release from Triggers and from the set responses to them is a paradigm-shift.

Paradigms are embedded views of the world around us, compiled by each of us according to our adopted Belief Systems and living circumstances. Everyone's paradigms are unique to them. Paradigms show us the world as we want to see it, which may not be as it truly is. They filter out information and channel us into looking at things and circumstances through a pre-set view-screen solely determined by the individual. In simple terms, you cannot see something if you're unwilling to acknowledge its existence.

A paradigm-shift is the conscious changing of how you view or experience something within the world. It means: to change your pre-set response to specific information sets into a more open and inclusive view of all the information reaching you, without judgement or pre-conditioning of its meaning.

Tool Seven is a swift and straight-forward technique to close on Triggers.

So far you have identified and confronted some of your specific Triggers. You have put forward desirable alternatives to the way they have made you behave in the past.

Now it is time to release your Self from these Triggers.

By applying your new responses to known Triggers and experiencing the different feelings that come with those new responses, you are beginning to take ownership of the Triggers themselves.

If you are willing enough and honest enough to take them on board and claim them as your own, then you are effectively freeing your Self from them forever.

This is a fundamental shift away from your embedded Belief System that pre-programs your responses to the Trigger situations. It is now a case of you being open to choosing new alternatives. Trying them on, finding those that fit best for the current You.

The old entrenched behaviours can be discarded in favour of more relevant and meaningful ones; ones that are pertinent to today, not just to yesterday.


**EXERCISE:**

Take ten minutes to identify a specific Trigger that occurs frequently within your life.

Examine it for its nature, content and source. Ask yourself why it has the power to trigger you. Where did that perception of its ability to trigger you really come from?

Identify and acknowledge the deep-seated paradigm that causes you to react the way that you do to that Trigger. Write down how you will deal with that paradigm-based reaction going forward, now that you have recognized it for what it truly is – just a set of unwanted pre-programmed responses.

# TOOL # 8

## BARRIERS RECOGNITION

One of the most common Barriers we all face encompasses self-sabotage, lack of self-love, lack of determination and focus, lack of faith in one's Self.

In this exercise you are required to honestly ask yourself to identify what are the patterns of thinking and behaviours that prevent you from moving on into a more positive life.

What aspects of your personality are so deeply rooted and entrenched within you that they automatically create negative thoughts and behaviours? Are they vested in you, caused by past events? Do you really still need these kinds of thoughts and behaviours in order to live your life in a positive and stress-free manner?

For example; perhaps you grew up in a dysfunctional home or environment, but that doesn't preclude you from pursuing a better life. All it takes is one straight-forward decision: to change your mind about who you think you are.

Many times these factors and behaviours are a consequence of your upbringing and/or sharing of an environment where such behaviours are commonplace and become your own norm. Plain and simple; they are learned behaviours. A common symptom of this is that we often feel as if we don't deserve happiness or success, for whatever reason.

The pivotal point to remember is that, as soon as you decide to change your mind, your life will change. You truly hold the key to your own destiny. It's such a simple thing to do. When you make a conscious decision not to be a victim of your own circumstance that you now recognize you're responsible for, you can turn around your own life.

When you give yourself permission to live out your true purpose, you inadvertently give others around you the same permission. It creates a ripple effect. It's not a conscious thing, but a natural phenomenon, because everything really is connected. We are all connected.

Having previously explored who you are and identifying unnecessary negative thinking and behaviours picked up in your life's journey, we now apply the Tool used for identifying Barriers to you achieving and connecting to your purpose.

The level of honesty required to ask this question of yourself and answer it truthfully is immense.

This is you helping you, in the deepest sense.

By recognizing the barriers and blockages to being your own positive Self and to reaching proper fulfilment in your life, it begins to release you from repeating the negative thinking and behaviours you identified when you listed your twenty dislikes about yourself.

You need to ask why you held onto and retained those specific thinking patterns and behaviours. What purposes do they truly serve in making your life a better place to be, if any?

If you divest of these, will getting rid of them improve who you are and improve how you live your life?

Let's find out.

This is a meditative exercise. It can be quite healing as you begin to write it out. By writing this out, you can begin to identify certain self-sabotaging thinking patterns and behaviours that can be blockages to living your true purpose.

**EXERCISE:**

I have identified the following barriers....

# TOOL # 9

## BELIEF SYSTEMS

These are closely linked to paradigms, in that Belief Systems create a framework for the world we live in. They set boundaries of behaviour and provide rules and guidelines for how to behave and interact with our respective environments.

Belief Systems are formed based on many factors, such as where you are born, the societal norms within which you are raised, the environment, the country, religious beliefs, racial ethnicity, etc.

Holding on to Belief Systems creates judgement. You end up perpetually measuring all behaviours against a set of 'standards' and expected activities. Those that do not measure up are not considered acceptable, leading to rejection thereof. By holding true to pre-set belief systems, you limit your own true self.

Previously, in Tool Seven, we briefly mentioned 'Belief Systems' with regard to pre-programmed behaviours and responses.

Belief Systems are mental constructs and value sets that underpin how each of us views the world and guides how we interact with it. They are the rules or guidelines, if you will, that we adopt internally to help us steer our path through life.

By their very nature, Belief Systems are what underpin our Triggers. Your Belief Systems filter information to categorize it; it determines what things are acceptable and flags those that are unacceptable to you. Belief Systems rank certain unacceptable or uncomfortable behaviours and events as requiring specific responses.

They are embedded in your psyche. They help you make sense of the external world, by framing everyday life events to extract order from chaos.

Tool Nine in the Self Repair Toolkit is an exercise in identifying when Belief Systems have migrated from useful mental constructs to being Barriers to developing, growing and evolving as a person.

We pose the question, "When do Belief Systems become negative constraints?"

## EXERCISE:

Identify two core Belief Systems that you hold dear to you. Write them down. Examine them to determine how/where/when you acquired these as part of your daily paradigms set that you live by.

Question whether they are necessary for you to live your life. Write down two possible alternatives to each Belief System. Now imagine a day in your life using either of these alternatives

.

# TOOL # 10

## WHO AM I?

For many of us, this is a question that can be answered in many different ways. The idea here is to write down, 'Who am I?', to progress beyond the accepted norm of labels ['mother', 'daughter', 'husband', 'son', etc.] and to see where you finally arrive. It is okay to start with those labels to give you a direction, but you must move beyond them to tap into who you really are.

By completing this exercise, it should help to identify that which you are not. In other words, there is a perception that you are your body, your thoughts, your feelings, your emotions, your breath, etc., but you are the one observing those. You are the only constant that is observing all those fluctuations that those perceptions give rise to.

The key to this exercise is to connect to your source; to your limitless Self. You will know that you have connected when you noticeably become less attached to and invested in the above perceptions.

For example, if you come up with a thought; try not to act on that thought, and see what happens; the same with a feeling. Try not to attach to a negative or positive thought or feeling. After some time of observation, you should notice that everything is passing [all thoughts, all emotions] like a cloud passing across the face of the sky. It's there, but you don't really own it. Why? Because you can only own it when you act upon it. That would create a reaction and trap you in a cycle of repeat behaviours, because you would inevitably be reinforcing those thought patterns/feelings/behaviours.

There is a lot of power rooted in observation. Without changing anything, through just observing over time, you will notice that the patterns of feelings/behaviours fall away, because they are no longer being reinforced by you taking action upon them.

This is a twenty minutes' exercise; a meditation on the Self. Be truthful and true to yourself.

**WHAT TO DO:** Go back over your life story. Look at it from a cold impassionate perspective. Does what you created properly cover your life story? Even after just having composed it, did it truly reflect 'you'? Be honest. Once you have done this, you are prepared for undertaking the exercise of 'Who am I?'

## WHY DO IT:

In applying this tool, you face the most basic and fundamental question anyone can ask of themselves; 'Who am I?'

Undertaking this exercise honestly will help you to identify with how you perceive and see yourself.

It is a broad scoped question that can move you to begin looking at yourself in an aspect of infiniteness; as an unending being. You are strongly encouraged to try to frame this exercise from the viewpoint of you being an on-going entity that exists in the now and has the capacity to perpetuate well beyond that.

By addressing the question of 'Who am I?' you unlock the potential of who you are.

Each of us is multi-faceted and multi-dimensional. A person is a virtually limitless being, comprising more than just the sum of their intellect. You are more than your intellect.

## EXERCISE:

I am....

# TOOL # 11

## PERMISSIONS

Tool Eleven deals with 'Permissions'. This Tool is partly about contemplating how you view things in your life. It's also about changing your thinking and taking responsibility for those things under your power and control.

Permissions relate to the moments in your life when you give up control over situations and events to others. They are deeply rooted in how you automatically apply your Belief Systems within everyday life.

To be affected by someone or something, you have to give conscious or sub-conscious permission to that person or thing to allow it to affect you [positively or negatively].

For example, a Trigger event occurs when someone calls you 'two-faced'.

If you don't truly believe that, then it has almost zero effect on you, positively or negatively. However, if you deep down believe it, then you are affected by it. In order to get beyond the impact, you need to take responsibility for it. That means; you accept within yourself that it's what you are, who you are. You do behave that way. You cause yourself to behave that way. It's your way of thinking; it's your behaviour. So own it. Be responsible for being so-called 'two-faced'.

By doing this, you immediately put power back into your own hands. You are not scrambling to deflect or defend against something that you inherently already believe to be true. You are now able to focus on dealing with it on your own terms, without having to take aim at the person describing it to you.

Through accessing your 'dormant power', (the underlying capacity within you to take responsibility and control over your thinking, actions and responses) it releases you AND the other person from any conflict or negative relationship arising from the Trigger event. Releasing is the consequence of dealing with Permissions.

Understanding Permissions is about having compassion for yourself in having that specific trait, or condition, which is the subject of the Trigger event. In immediately recognizing that it is not about the other person instigating the Trigger event, but wholly about who and what you are, you release that person from the event. It's not theirs; it's yours. You immediately become powerful by acknowledging it and not allowing someone else to hurt you through pointing it out openly.

# TOOL # 12

## VISIONING

Tool Twelve is about Visioning; forward focus. It is an exercise in direction-setting for the Self. It is not something that we urge you to do immediately, if you are still working through your understanding of your Belief Systems and Permissions, but it is an invaluable tool in determining where you are directing your true Self going forward.

You are in the NOW. That is first and foremost what counts for you; being in the moment.

However, there is also a desire to use your power to create and build upon your better Self.

**EXAMPLE:**

Refer to Deborah's personal visioning experience on her cloud based SRT audio support at https://www.soundcloud.com/deborah-small-1

**EXERCISE:**

Now that you control your power, unhindered by negative Triggers, Belief Systems and Permissions, you are in a place in your life that is clear and can allow you to focus forward.

The following tools provide you with two approaches to Visioning.

Deborah's example from her own personal Visioning was a present-to-future journey. That is the first kind of Visioning tool you can explore. It starts in the present and moves forward from there.

Present-to-Future Visioning Tool:

1. Determine your time line; we suggest you start small with bite-sized short-ranged time periods [a month, six months, a year].
2. Focus on Self; what part of your life do you feel is most in need of change going forward?
3. Deal with any pain in that part of your life first; address those issues as a priority in your Visioning.
4. Write down what the pain or hurt being felt consists of. Identify why you are experiencing it.
5. Set out in your mind how you want the Vision to look, beyond the painful present to the changed state; write down what is the destination.
6. How will you know you have arrived at it? What are the changes you will be looking for? Write them down.
7. Ask yourself whether the destination is something that is wanted by you. Will you feel comfortable being there? It's important that your destination is a desirable one. It is a motivator to making your Vision a reality.
8. Plan how you believe you can move to that destination; what are the steps you will need to put in place to make it happen? Note all of them down; be detailed. Note when they should be occurring; this provides the time line with urgency. This 'urgency' becomes a form of what is known as 'creative tension'. It's quite amazing how that creative tension empowers you to resolve some of the obstacles to achieving your Vision.

Remember, you only need your Self to be engaged in the Visioning process; everything comes from you. Mantras help, writing down all aspects of your Visioning also helps. It's about what you are comfortable with.

The second is another approach in how to engage in Visioning. It is a simple future-back-planning tool to aid you in Visioning - setting your direction for moving forward through your life. It takes you to the destination first, then you ask yourself how you managed to get there.

Please follow these steps:

1. Select a time in the future; a month, a year, five years – you choose.
2. See yourself in a specific place within that time. Describe it in detail as if you are standing there and looking around yourself.
3. What does that place/location look like? What are the sights, sounds, aromas?
4. Who else is there? Friends, strangers, loved ones?
5. What are you doing at that time, in that place?
6. How does it feel to be there? Relaxed, exciting, peaceful?
7. Now take a moment in that future place to ask yourself, "How did I get here?"
8. Start to write down how you believe you were able to have arrived at that place

and state of being in that future. What were the milestone events [painful or otherwise] or circumstances that contributed to you having arrived at that place and time?

9. Track these events moving back in time to the present. Keep aware of what changes as you journey back to your present. Certain things do tend to be sequential, so look for linked events where possible, one following the other. By doing this, you are mapping your Visioning process and determining what needs to happen to get to that desired future state. This provides you with a kind of road map of how to get to your envisioned future state.

For further audio support please visit Deborah's SoundCloud page at
https://www.soundcloud.com/deborah-small-1

## WITH THANKS

*It is my sincere hope that you will, by having gone through this process openly and honestly, have challenged yourself; at the very least to think and do things differently from before. If so, visible change has taken place.*

*The thing to remember is; your presence, your attention and whatever you bring your attention to, is where the true empowerment lies.*

*To be stuck within old paradigms would be counter-beneficial to your progress and to your journey to Self. The past is gone, dead. The future has not arrived yet. You only have the present.*

*The gift of the present is that everything can be new; all possibilities exist in the NOW. This depends on how successfully you are able to let go of the past and/or the future.*

*Your ability to stay "present" is what ultimately creates your success in anything with anything.*

*I wish you an exciting, fulfilling, infinite and all-encompassing NOW.*

**WITH LOVE & LIGHT**

***DEBORAH SMALL***

## ABOUT THE TOOLKIT CREATOR

Deborah is an internationally acknowledged expert practitioner within the field of life healing. She has twenty years of practical experience gained in Asia, Africa, Middle East, Europe, Australasia and North America. She holds qualifications as; Integrative Reprogramming Technique ['IRT'] facilitator, Yoga Instructor, Nutritionist and instructor of advanced breathing techniques for self-healing. She is also a practiced and experienced group and retreats facilitator. Deborah holds a degree in Psychology from the University of British Columbia.

Visit Deborah's website - https://www.blissfullpath.com/

Made in the USA
Columbia, SC
19 March 2018